the guide to owning a
Parakeet

John Bales

Photo Credits

Larry Allan: 10
Joan Balzarini: 7 (top), 33, 53, 56
Susan Chamberlain: 32
Isabelle Francais: 15, 16, 30, 38, 47, 51, 60
Michael Gilroy: 9, 12 (top), 18, 19 (top), 21, 52
Eric Ilasenko: 4
Bonnie Jay: 5, 8, 19 (bottom), 29, 41, 43, 48, 55, 61
Robert Pearcy: 25
Lara Stern: 14, 44 (top), 62
John Tyson: 7 (bottom), 12 (bottom), 36, 45, 49, 57, 58, 59

T.F.H. Publications, Inc.
One TFH Plaza
Third and Union Avenues
Neptune City, NJ 07753

This book has been published with the intent to provide accurate and authoritative information in regard to the subject matter within. While every precaution has been taken in preparation of this book, the publisher and author assume no responsibility for errors or omissions. Neither is any liability assumed for damages resulting from the use of the information herein.

ISBN 0-7938-2008-1

www.tfhpublications.com

Contents

Introducing the Parakeet

The parakeet has captivated the imagination of humans for centuries and is now firmly established as one of the world's most popular pets. In fact, the parakeet is the most popular companion bird in the US and the world.

It's easy to understand why the parakeet is so popular. For one thing, no other bird is available in such a

The parakeet is the most popular companion bird in the US.

The total body length of an adult parakeet is approximately 6 inches.

wide range of colors. This fact alone accounts for the thousands of enthusiasts who devote their energies to both improving and adding to the possible color mutations that can develop. Parakeets are also extremely hardy birds that are easy to feed and breed. Furthermore, parakeets are the ideal family pet. They are great for children, and most are quite talkative.

PARAKEET ORIGINS AND HISTORY

In many parts of the world, parakeets are also called "budgerigars," or "budgies" for short. This comes from the Aboriginal Australians' word for

The wild parakeet is green, so all other colors are actually mutations.

THE GUIDE TO OWNING A PARAKEET

Parakeets are hardy birds that make ideal family pets.

this bird, *betchegara*. The parakeet's scientific name is *Melopsittacus undulates*, and parakeets are actually members of the parrot family, Psittacidae. Parakeets are originally from the Australian outback and still inhabit the interior of Australia, but pet parakeets are bred in captivity, not imported from the wild.

In the wild, the parakeet groups with thousands of his own kind in large migratory flocks. These flocks follow watercourses and live off wild grasses, seeds, and vegetation found on dry grasslands. Wild parakeets eat in the morning, roost at midday, and eat again in the late afternoon before returning to the roost area in the

Parakeets are famous for their vocalizations. They frequently talk, sing, and mimic words and sounds.

Parakeets come in more than 70 colors and can live to be about 12 to 15 years old if provided with the proper care and environment.

evening. The roost area is usually a large tree, in which all members of the flock will meet daily.

APPEARANCE

The total body length of a parakeet is approximately 6 inches, and adults weigh less than 1 ounce.

Parakeets now come in more than 70 colors, and you can expect that number to increase as more colors develop. The wild budgie is green, so all other colors are called "muta-tions." You will probably only find a few of these colors available, as many of the colors are limited to breeders and exhibitors. Some of the common colors are shades of green, blue, yellow (lutino), and pied (a mixture of two colors).

LIFESPAN

Parakeets are very hardy birds and can live to be about 12 to 15 years old if given proper care and a balanced diet.

Parakeets are good parents and produce about four to eight young in each clutch. Most pairs hatch out their babies in only 18 to 21 days and wean them in only four to five weeks. In the wild, the breeding cycle is controlled by rainfall and the availability of food, but in captivity, the breeding cycle must be controlled.

Vocalizations

Parakeets are famous for their ability to talk and vocalize. They are excellent talkers and will frequently mimic words and sounds, though it is perfectly normal for a parakeet not to talk. Parakeets also frequently sing, and their song is a rather pleasant sound.

Overall, parakeets are affectionate, friendly birds that will make a great addition to any family.

Choosing a Parakeet

Purchasing a parakeet as a pet is not as simple as it may first appear. Caring for a parakeet is a serious responsibility. You must, of course, be committed to the care of any pet, but with a bird as friendly and as intelligent as a parakeet, that care includes a lot of time beyond just

Because parakeets are social birds, you may want to consider buying a pair or group of parakeets.

You should be prepared for the expenses and care involved in parakeet ownership before obtaining one of these birds as your companion.

providing a clean cage, food, and water. Therefore, it is best to be prepared for all of the responsibilities that come with parakeet ownership and to know what to look for when deciding on the perfect parakeet for your home and family.

IS THE PARAKEET RIGHT FOR YOU?
Socialization

Parakeets are intelligent and social creatures. Therefore, parakeets need attention and frequent social interaction. You must be prepared to spend a lot of time with your bird and provide him with enough stimulation so that he does not get bored. This may mean keeping more than one para-

Parakeets have very friendly temperaments, and they get along with many other small bird species, such as cockatiels.

THE GUIDE TO OWNING A PARAKEET

Make sure that all members of your household will enjoy having a parakeet as a pet.

keet or paying a great deal of time and attention to a single parakeet. This also entails allowing your parakeet to have time outside of his cage on a daily basis.

Expenses and Care Requirements

While providing for your parakeet's emotional and social needs is probably most important, you also need to be prepared for the more basic responsibilities as well. Your parakeet will need to be fed twice a day, and in order to receive a healthy diet, he will need more than just seeds or pellets—he will need plenty of fruits, vegetables, and other fresh foods as well.

Your parakeet will need a cage and all of the other accessories required. Most of these are one-time purchases, however, so you will only have to budget for this expense in the beginning.

You also need to account for the cost of veterinary visits. You should take your parakeet to the veterinarian for an initial health evaluation within the first few days of obtaining him, and he will also need regular checkups thereafter. Even if your parakeet never becomes sick, you should take him to his avian veterinarian at least once a year for a checkup.

Parakeets and Children

Because they have such friendly temperaments, parakeets are great companions for children, as long as parents are willing to accept responsibility for the bird's care as well. If you decide to get a parakeet for your

Parakeets of any age make great pets, though young birds are easier to hand-tame and train.

The male parakeet can be distinguished by his blue cere, as depicted on this male.

child, carefully review all of the responsibilities involved with caring for the bird, such as feeding, water, cage cleaning, etc. Also make sure the child understands that a parakeet is a living, breathing creature that requires love, positive attention, and respect. Be clear that the child should not poke or tease the bird or disturb him when he wants to be left alone. It's also a good idea to supervise the child when the bird is out of the cage and to have the child ask for your permission before removing the bird from his cage for any reason.

Will a Parakeet Fit Into Your Lifestyle?

Another important consideration is whether a pet parakeet will fit into your lifestyle and your family. Do you

A healthy parakeet will appear alert and energetic and will have sleek, smooth feathers that lie flat against his body.

have other pets, such as cats or dogs, which may be potential threats to a parakeet? Will you be able to carefully supervise your parakeet when he is out of the cage? Do you have children or many people living in the house? Would they all be happy with having a parakeet in the house?

If you have considered all of these things and have decided you have everything required to provide a parakeet with the proper care and environment, you are now ready to bring a parakeet into your home!

A hand-raised parakeet is one that was hand-fed and reared by a human caregiver rather than his parents.

CHOOSING THE RIGHT PARAKEET FOR YOU

Selecting a Healthy Parakeet

A parakeet in good, healthy condition will be very alert and move from perch to perch quite freely. His eyes will be bright and round, and the feathers will be sleek and lie flat against the wings and body. There will be no sign of staining around the vent, and the cere will be clean, with no signs of mucus or discharge.

If a parakeet has a fluffed-up appearance or is sitting in a corner of the cage on the floor, he is probably ill. If the parakeet has patches of missing feathers or a deformed beak or leg, this is probably a sign of illness as well. Also, do not buy a parakeet from a shop or breeder that houses their birds in unclean, dirty conditions.

Age

The ideal age to acquire a parakeet as a pet is when he is approximately six weeks old. By this age, he should be feeding himself and will not be frightened when you want to handle him.

At six weeks of age, a baby parakeet appears to have large, dark eyes. This is because his white iris ring has not yet developed. It does not fully develop until about five months of age. Therefore, this ring is an indication of age.

Getting an older bird is just as wonderful, but an older pet may require more time and attention in order for him to bond with you.

Male or Female?

Male and female parakeets make equally good pets, though it is commonly stated that if you wish for your bird to talk and mimic words, a male bird is preferred. Female parakeets can also learn to talk, but the male is thought to be more inclined to do so.

You can tell the difference between a male and female because the cere (area above the beak) is blue on an adult male, while the cere on an adult hen is a brown or tan color. It is difficult to distinguish between the sexes when the parakeets are very young, however.

Hand-raised or Parent-raised?

A hand-raised raised baby is one who was taken away from his parents at an early age and reared on formula fed by a human in a syringe or spoon. These birds bond quickly with humans and are comfortable in a human environment.

It may be a good idea to choose a hand-raised baby parakeet. They are already hand-tamed, though they are rare and usually more expensive.

Parent-raised birds can be just as great as pets; however, you will have to take the time to hand-tame them yourself.

Parakeets of all colors make equally good pets.

Color

Color has no bearing on the pet potential of a parakeet. Parakeets of all color make equally good pets. There are numerous color varieties to choose from, but the price of more colorful parakeets will be slightly higher than that of a green or a blue, the more common colors.

Housing Your Parakeet

Just like humans, parakeets need a safe and secure place to call their home. Therefore, when choosing a cage for your parakeet, try to select one that will be more than a cage—choose one that will feel like a home.

You can do this by making sure the cage is the proper size, shape, and

Large square or rectangular cages with a simple design are the best type of parakeet housing.

Your parakeet's cage should be large enough for him to be able to fly from one end to another.

material and is positioned in an appropriate location. Your parakeet's cage should be clean, safe, and comfortable.

THE CAGE

Size and Shape

How big should the cage be? Buy the largest cage you can afford. You actually don't need to buy a cage that is very tall, but horizontal space is a must.

Therefore, the best cage shape to buy is a large square or rectangle-shaped cage. Round cages are not preferred no matter how large because they don't provide any corners—corners make parakeets feel safe and secure. Also, stay away from

It's best to give your parakeet a cage with a relatively simple design.

The cage should be placed in a warm, safe, active place where your parakeet will feel like a part of the family.

any elaborate or ornately designed cages—the abstract parts can be dangerous.

At the very least, the cage should be large enough so the bird can fly from one end to the other. It is cruel to confine a bird as active as a parakeet to a cage so small that he can merely hop from perch to perch. There are many different cages on the market that are designated as parakeet cages specifically, but many of these are too small. Of course, a parakeet is not very large, so a 24-inch cage provides ample room for him to fly. If you allow the bird some time outside the cage every day, a smaller cage can suffice, because your pet will get plenty of flying exercise when he is free in the room.

Cage Material

The best material for your parakeet's cage is uncoated steel or wrought iron. Plastic on a metal cage is acceptable, but it's best not to buy a cage that has any paint or coating covering it—your parakeet may chew on this coating, and it can be highly toxic.

Cage Flooring

Your parakeet's cage should have a slide-out tray at the bottom to make cleaning easy and quick. Newspaper is probably the best thing you can use to line the tray. The best arrangement is to have a wire floor above the tray so that the bird does not have access

Natural branches are good choices for perches because their size and shape vary; they are also great for chewing.

is going on around him and should be part of the action of your family's everyday activities. However, make sure he is not in a place that has too much activity, such as a hallway or kitchen. You want your parakeet to feel connected but not stressed.

CAGE ACCESSORIES

Perches

There are many types of perches available—wood, plastic, braided rope, natural, and even concrete for keeping toenails and beaks trimmed. The important thing is to have perches of different diameters so that the bird's feet get natural exercise.

to it. This is easier said than done, however, and often a persistent bird can get to the newspaper anyway.

Where to Place the Cage

The cage should be placed where it is free from drafts, and it should be in a well-lit position. However, it's best not to place the cage in the direct sun, which can overheat the cage and your parakeet inside. Your parakeet must always be able to move into the shade if he so desires.

You should also place the cage in a room where your parakeet will feel he is a part of the family. Your parakeet should be able to see everything that

Braided rope makes a great perch for parakeets.

Heavy, round crock-style dishes are the most sturdy and convenient for providing your parakeet with food and water.

Many owners prefer natural branches. Aside from being non-uniform in size, they offer twigs and bark for the birds to chew on, which they love to do. If you have a place where you can gather natural branches, this is ideal, but make sure that the trees you select are not poisonous to your bird and have not been sprayed with insecticides. Safe trees include maple, willow, and fruit trees.

Toys

Even if you have more than one parakeet, toys are essential to keep them entertained. Parakeets are extremely intelligent birds and need constant mental stimulation.

Parakeets are very active and love swings, ladders, and other objects on which they can climb.

THE GUIDE TO OWNING A PARAKEET

Mirrors are favorite toys of parakeets, who will frequently sing, talk, and perform for a mirror.

Aviaries are great housing choices if you would like to get a group of birds.

Your pet store will have a large assortment of bird toys that are safe. Avoid toys with loops or holes in which the bird could get his head, wing, or toes caught. A little parakeet's beak is not able to destroy toys the way a large parrot can, but whittling and biting are important to keeping any bird's beak in shape, so you must be sure to provide wooden toys (or even little blocks of scrap wood) for them to chew.

Parakeets are active acrobats and will greatly appreciate playing on swings, ladders, ropes, chains, and other climbing apparatus. Parakeets also love mirrors. They will sing to a mirror, talk to a mirror, and perform to a mirror. Mirrors are especially good entertainment for single parakeets.

Remember to change the bird's toys often to prevent boredom. This does not mean you have to buy a new toy once a week. Simply rotate them regularly, and the old toys that have been stored for a while will seem "new."

Food and Water Cups

Heavy, round, crock-style dishes are the best choices for serving food and water to your parakeet. Ceramic and stainless steel are the best materials because they are easy to clean and heavy enough so that your parakeets cannot easily knock them over. Stay away from plastic because it is not sturdy enough, and also stay away from square or rectangle-shaped dishes—the corners are very difficult to clean thoroughly and can retain bacteria.

It's important to give your parakeet playtime outside of the cage on a daily basis, no matter how large his cage is.

The best aviary base is concrete or cement, which can be easily decorated and cleaned.

No matter how hard you try, a water bowl will usually be dirty with seed hulls, bits of food, pieces of paper, and bird droppings. Therefore, it is necessary to change your bird's water at least once a day. You should also thoroughly clean the food and water dishes at least once a week. It's a good idea to buy two sets of each dish so that you can use one set while the other is being cleaned.

Another solution is a water bottle. It is easy to train a parakeet to drink from a bottle. Parakeets are naturally curious, and if you buy a bottle specif-ically made for birds, the bottle will probably have a bright-red regulator ball in the tube, which is usually suffi-cient to attract the bird's attention. Once the bird has poked the ball and gotten a drop of water, he will know where to get a drink. Just watch to be certain he is drinking.

Do not simply fill the bottle and for-get about it. Every day when you clean the cage, you should tap or squeeze the bottle to make sure a drop comes out, and every few days you must take it off the cage and clean it thoroughly. In fact, having two bottles and rotating them is rec-ommended. Let each dry completely after you clean it. This helps prevent bacteria from growing in it.

Baths

Parakeets love baths, so it's a good idea to get some kind of bath for your bird's cage. Pet stores will have numerous styles and sizes of bird-baths for your parakeet. Also be warned that parakeets love baths so much that they may bathe in their water dishes. Therefore, clean your bird's water dish often, and change his bath water often as well.

AVIARIES

Another option is to house your parakeet in an aviary. Aviaries are great if you would like to get a group of parakeets or if you would like to house your parakeet with other similarly sized bird species. You can purchase a ready-made aviary, build your own aviary, or have an aviary built for you. Either way, you need to obtain the proper building permits in order to create such a structure on your property.

An aviary can be designed in many ways, and the only real limiting factor is your imagination. However, there are certain needs that all aviaries have in common. For instance, an aviary must be secure enough to keep the birds in but unwanted visitors out. There should also be some form of shelter attached so your parakeets can retreat there in the case of inclement weather. Finally, it must be arranged so that you can complete daily feeding and cleaning chores in a degree of comfort. Given these basics, the size and design of your aviary will largely be a matter of finances, space, and individual inclination.

Planning the Aviary Construction

The first stage of aviary construction is to select a suitable site and then prepare a detailed ground plan, which includes the shelter and its internal arrangements. This will show you exactly how your plans will work out in the space available. It is much easier to make alterations than to have to do them once construction is underway. This is also the time when you should obtain the proper building permits for the structure.

The overall size of an aviary will depend on the amount of space and expense allotted for the construction and how many parakeets or other species you will be housing.

Aviary perches should be natural branches and/or dowels of various shapes and sizes.

Ideally, the aviary site should be positioned to face the early morning sun. A backdrop of trees will help provide protection to an aviary from heavy winds. However, building an aviary under overhanging branches should be avoided; not only are the leaves messy when they shed in the fall, but some types can also emit toxic substances.

The chosen site should be in full view of your home so that services, such as water and electricity, can be easily installed. These services, of course, are not essential, but they certainly make routine chores more convenient.

The Aviary Floor

There are several types of material you can have as flooring for your aviary. The first option and the least expensive is to simply leave the bare earth as the aviary floor. However, the inexpensive price is probably the only advantage to a bare-earth floor. After rain has fallen, the base becomes a sea of mud, and weeds will eventually appear all over. More importantly, a bare-earth floor is actually dangerous because predators can easily dig through and get inside the aviary, leaving your parakeets vulnerable.

Therefore, the best aviary base is concrete or cement, which can be cleaned and hosed down easily. For decoration, you can easily add a layer of gravel over the concrete, which should be hosed down and raked each week.

Aviary Size and Shape

The height of the aviary should be no less than 6.5 feet (2 meters). Otherwise, the roofline will interfere with your view and access of the birds. The overall size of the aviary will obviously depend on available space and expenses allotted to the purchase. To allow your parakeets to get the most enjoyment and benefit from the aviary, allow as much flight room as possible. Length is far more important than width for parakeets.

Most aviaries tend to be of a simple rectangular box shape (this being the easiest to construct.) However, a little creativity can offer a far more pleasing sight.

For example, a slope on the roofline from the shelter downward adds appeal, or better yet is to have the slope going upward from the shelter, as the birds always prefer to perch at the highest point, and thus (given suitable perches) they are encouraged to the front of the aviary where they are better viewed. Circular aviaries and "L" shaped aviaries are gaining in popularity, though they are more costly to build.

Safety Porch

A safety porch should definitely be considered for an aviary of any design. A safety porch is simply a separate section enclosed in wiremesh that has one door as an entrance to the aviary, and another door that serves as an exit. With a safety porch, you will open a door that leads to the porch, close that door behind you, and then enter the aviary from the porch. This way, none of your parakeets can escape when you open the aviary door, because they will actually only be entering into the safety porch. This is an extremely valuable addition to your aviary. It's also a good idea to have the doors spring-loaded so that they won't be left open by accident.

If the aviary is small, the porch should be added externally so as not to take up any of the flight area. Should no porch be possible, then it is advised that the aviary door be lower than normal height. This will mean bending down to enter, but this is better than losing your parakeets.

Shelters and Bird Rooms

The shelter end of an aviary is a wood or brick-built structure where the birds will return to each night in order to roost. More commonly seen is a totally enclosed shelter combined with a service area, which contains cages, a storage area for food, and other requirements, thus becoming a bird room.

The building should have a sloping roof to take away rainwater, and guttering for this purpose is also recommended. The roof should have an outer protective coat of roofing felt over the wood, and it is advisable to line the internal walls and ceiling with plasterboard, plywood, or similar material. If extra insulation is required, then a suitable material can

As with cage housing, accessorize an aviary with plenty of toys and perches.

be placed between the outer and inner walls, usually some form of fiberglass wool.

The bird room should allow as much light as possible, as parakeets do not like entering darkened places. Therefore, at least one window should be incorporated. Plan the room so that no space is wasted and so that shelves are at the appropriate heights for ease of use.

Services for the Aviary

The availability of both electricity and water to a bird room are most useful, as these take much of the hard work out of the chores. Electricity should be installed professionally so that it's safe and conforms to local laws and regulations. Any cabling that might be exposed to your parakeets is better encased in conduit.

A faucet in the bird room is very handy, and available hot water for washing purposes is an extra luxury.

AVIARY ACCESSORIES

After having the aviary built or placed, the final task is to furnish the aviary with the proper accessories. The essentials needed are perches, food and water containers, and a bath.

Perches

Aviary perches should either be natural branches or dowels of various shapes and sizes. Branches of fruit trees are the favored choice among many parakeet owners, though other tree branches are acceptable as long as they are safe for birds and not sprayed with toxic chemical insecticides. Branches should have a wide range of sizes in order to give your parakeets' feet a suitable amount of exercise.

Make sure that you do not put too many branches in the aviary, because this reduces the flight area. In order to keep your parakeets in fit condition, the flight area should be as spacious as possible. Place the branches at either end of the aviary and add extras elsewhere only if the area is large enough.

Food and Water Dishes

As with cages, the best way to give food and water to your parakeets is with heavy, round crock-style dishes. You can also try the gravity-fed water bottles as long as you check them often to make sure they are not clogged.

You can either make tables for the food containers, or the bowls can be placed on the shelter floor or shelves made for this purpose. Do not place the food or water containers below a perch or they can be fouled easily.

Baths

In the wild, parakeets bathe in shallow ponds rather than in the rain. Therefore, the inclusion of a shallow container sunk into the aviary floor will enable your parakeets to keep their feathers well preened. They will also drink from this, so it is important to keep this pool free of excessive debris.

Feeding Your Parakeet

Parakeets are known as hardbills, which means that the base of their diet consists of seed and/or grain. However, a parakeet cannot stay healthy on seed alone. Like humans, parakeets need a balanced diet with a lot of variety. While the bulk of your parakeet's diet can be a quality seed

In order to provide your parakeet with a balanced diet, a good ratio is 25-percent pellets, 25-percent seeds, and 50-percent fruits, vegetables, and other healthy foods.

mix and/or a specially formulated pellet, your parakeet's diet still should be supplemented with other healthy foods. A good ratio is 25-percent pellets, 25-percent seeds, and 50-percent fruits, vegetables, and other healthy foods.

PELLETS

Pellets are small, compressed food bits that come in various shapes and sizes, which contain many of the vitamins and nutrients that are necessary for your bird's health. Pellets can come in a variety of colors and flavors, while others are plain and uniform in shape and color. Though they are nutritious, some of the

Grains, legumes, and other healthy foods should be included in your parakeet's diet.

nutrients can be lost in processing, and pellets are usually not specifically formulated for the dietary needs of individual breeds. Pellets are a decent base diet, but they still need to be supplemented with other healthy foods.

SEEDS

There are many seed mixes available that are formulated specifically for parakeets. Sunflower seeds are a great treat, but because they are fatty, they should only be fed occasionally and should not make up a bulk of the seed mix. As with pellets, supplement seeds with lots of fruits, vegetables, and other healthy foods. Parakeets can easily become interested only in seed, so it is important to introduce your parakeet to a wide variety of healthy foods from the beginning.

FRUITS AND VEGETABLES

If you base the diet on a seed mix or pellets, you should supplement with fruits and vegetables every day. With a pelleted diet you do not need to be as consistent, though there is no harm in offering these foods on a daily basis. You can feed your bird any fruit or vegetable suitable for human consumption except avocados, which are reported to be toxic to birds.

The key is variety. Feed lots of different foods, taking advantage of what is in season. Especially nutritious

Fruits and vegetables are essential to your parakeet's daily diet, even if you feed him seeds or pellets.

are dark-green leafy vegetables and orange vegetables. Raw vegetables have the most vitamins; they can be chopped, grated, or fed as whole pieces.

EGGS

Eggs are a great food for birds. They contain many nutrients, especially the shell, which parakeets will eat heartily. When feeding the egg with the shell to your parakeet, make sure to wash the shell thoroughly first, because it can harbor bacteria.

The only drawback to eggs is that they are too rich and fatty to feed every day. Try to feed eggs about once a week. The preferred method is to hard-boil the eggs, then use a sharp knife to slice them lengthwise in half without removing the shell.

OTHER HEALTHY FOODS

Grains and legumes of all kinds are ideal foods for parakeets. Brown rice, dry beans, and pasta can be cooked until tender and fed as-is or mixed with vegetables or bread.

Many people bake "birdy bread," which is simply a cornbread recipe with the addition of things such as sunflower seeds and green vegetables. Regular whole-grain breads are also relished by parakeets and provide a lot of nutrition.

Many parakeet owners also provide

Spray millet is a treat that most parakeets love and will happily enjoy eating.

Treats are acceptable on occasion and serve as great training rewards.

mineral blocks and cuttlebones as treats. The treats are particularly beneficial because they entertain your bird by providing hours of chewing while also providing some valuable minerals.

Remember that the more variety you provide, the better the diet will be, and the more likely your pet will be to try new foods when you offer them.

TREATS

Treats are acceptable on occasion and are great to use as rewards when training.

Sunflower seeds are a real favorite. Your bird will soon let you know what foods he particularly likes. One thing relished by almost all birds is spray millet. This is millet dried in its natural form, still on the stem, and birds go crazy for it.

Never feed your parakeet caffeine (in coffee, tea, chocolate, or cola) or salt, and an excess of sugar or fat should not be given to your bird either.

WATER

Water should be available for your parakeet at all times. Individuals vary in the amounts they drink, but all parakeets need plenty of fresh water. Make sure to change your parakeet's water container at least once a day, preferably at least twice a day.

Grooming Your Parakeet

Grooming is very important to your parakeets, and they will feel their best if they are clean and their

Parakeets relish bathing, so provide your bird with a bath in his cage or offer him alternative bathing facilities.

feathers are groomed. Fortunately, parakeets are relatively easy to care for when it comes to grooming, because they will handle most of their grooming needs themselves. The only grooming tasks you'll really have to concern yourself with are bathing, nail trimming, and wing clipping (if you prefer to do this).

BATHING
Parakeets absolutely love to bathe, so you should provide your parakeet with some type of bath in his cage.

Your parakeet will decide when it is time for his bath, so all you need to do is provide him with the bird bath and fresh water in the bath.

NAIL CLIPPING
If they are not worn down with use, a parakeet's toenails will grow too long, which will interfere with his ability to

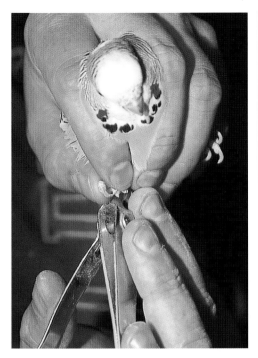

You will only need to clip your parakeet's toenails if they do not wear down naturally during normal activities.

get around and could prove dangerous if the nails get caught and entangled in something. If you do need to trim your parakeet's nails, you will need several supplies. You should have a towel to wrap your parakeet in during the trimming process, nail clippers (those made for humans should do fine), and styptic powder, in case the nail is cut too deeply and bleeds. It's also a good idea to have a nail file to smooth the edges after you cut.

You may want to enlist the aid of a helper while clipping your bird's nails. This person can hold your parakeet gently in a towel while you take on the task of clipping.

When the bird is secure, use a sharp nail clipper to cut the excess nail off.

Trim off only the tip of the nail where it is hooked. If you want to use a file, file each nail after you clip it.

The main concern with clipping the nails is that you avoid the quick—the blood vessel deep within the nail. If you should hit the vein, you will not be very deep into it, and a dab with a styptic pencil should stop any bleeding. Remember what the nail looks like at that point, and always trim just a little longer in the future.

WING CLIPPING

Wing clipping is a controversial topic—some people consider it absolutely essential, while others condemn it as mutilation. Those who

If you need to trim your parakeet's toenails, be careful to avoid the quick, the blood vessel inside the nail.

are in favor of wing clipping feel it keeps the parakeet safe from escaping or from encountering household dangers. Those who are against wing clipping feel it limits the bird's freedom and robs the parakeet of his natural flying abilities. The choice is up to you. Keep in mind that wing clipping does not hurt your bird at all, but it does inhibit his natural flying abilities.

Many bird owners trim their bird's wings when they first get him but let the feathers grow back with the next molt. By that time he is tamed, trained, and accustomed to his new home. Parakeets are so affectionate that if your bird was hand-raised, he will probably be so tame and bonded to humans that you will not need to clip his wings to control him.

If you decide to clip the wings, you should have your avian veterinarian or breeder show you how to do this. You may even want to have your parakeet's veterinarian handle the task every time, but you can do it yourself if you have been taught the correct way by your veterinarian. Wing clipping involves cutting the flight feathers with sharp scissors, straight across. It sounds simple, but you really do need a professional to show you how to do it first. Your parakeet can be easily injured during wing trimming, so it's important to see how it is done correctly.

You will most likely need a partner to aid you in this task. It's also important that you clip your parakeet's wings in a very well-lit area. You will need a towel to wrap your parakeet

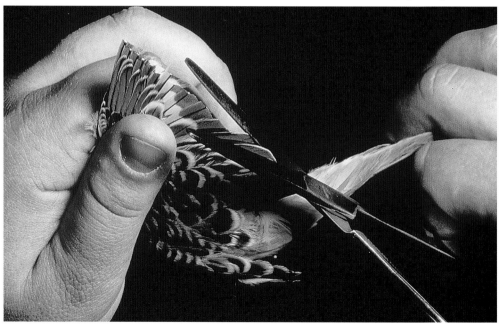

Wing clipping involves cutting your parakeet's flight feathers straight across with sharp scissors.

in, a pair of sharp scissors, styptic powder to stop any bleeding, and needle-nosed pliers (in case you have to pluck a broken blood feather.)

Gather your parakeet in his towel and have your partner hold him with one wing spread out. With your scissors, carefully and slowly cut the flight feathers, starting at the wing tips and working inward closer to your parakeet's body. Parakeets may need to have several flight feathers cut, though the number you cut depends on the size of your bird's body.

If you trim a blood feather (feathers that have not fully grown in yet), you will have to pluck it out with one quick motion and apply styptic powder to the area immediately to stop the bleeding. If the bleeding does not stop right away, apply some pressure to the area. If it still continues, a trip to the vet will be necessary. This is why it is often a good idea to simply have your veterinarian undertake this task for you.

Your parakeet will probably only need his wings clipped a few times a year. You may even decide to clip him in the beginning, while he is still getting used to your family and home, and then allow the wings to grow once he is more mature and adjusted.

Wing clipping keeps your bird safe and will not cause him pain, though many parakeet owners are still hesitant to clip their birds' wings.

IS BEAK TRIMMING NECESSARY?

Your parakeet's beak should wear down naturally from everyday activities, such as eating, chewing on toys and perches, and picking up objects with his beak. If your parakeet's beak is not wearing down naturally, there could be a problem. Therefore, you should take him to his avian veterinarian immediately. Never try to trim your parakeet's beak yourself. Only a professional should handle this task.

Taming and Training

Normally, parakeets that are purchased when they are about six weeks old are either already hand-tamed or can be easily hand-tamed.

Older birds can be hand-tamed as well, but it may take a bit more time and patience. Once your parakeet is hand-tamed and comfortable being

Hand-taming and training will be most successful if you are gentle and patient at all times.

When hand-taming and training your parakeet, conduct your sessions in a small, quiet room free of distractions.

handled, you can move on to other types of training.

HAND-TAMING YOUR PARAKEET

If your parakeet is not hand-tamed when you purchase him, you will need to hand-tame him yourself if you want to be able to hold him, play with him, or have him come to you after having time outside of his cage. If your parakeet is young, hand-taming will be fairly easy if you are patient and gentle at all times. It may take longer for older birds, but it will be worth the effort. The best time to begin hand-taming your parakeet is in the early evening after he has eaten and when he is less hyper and active. The room you choose should be quiet and free from dis-tractions (such as the television or other people). It should also be a fairly small and safe room, such as a bathroom, so that your parakeet will not injure himself or fly away when you take him out of the cage.

How to Hand-Tame Your Parakeet

Open the cage door and slowly move your index finger toward your parakeet inside the cage. He will mostly likely flutter away. Leave your hand in the cage for a few minutes and then withdraw it. Repeat this action a number of times, and even-tually your parakeet will not flutter away when you reach your hand toward him.

Next, slowly move your finger to your parakeet's lower abdomen, and

Once your bird is comfortable perching on your finger while inside of the cage, you can gradually bring him out of the cage while still perched on your finger.

he should hop onto your finger in an attempt to avoid it touching his abdomen. Do not try to bring your parakeet out of his cage at this time, however. Repeat this action many times over the course of a few days so that your parakeet feels comfortable perching on your finger.

Once your parakeet is comfortable perching on your finger inside the cage, you can then work on bringing him out of the cage. Have him perch onto your finger, and slowly bring your hand closer to the door. If he jumps off of your finger at some point as you bring him closer to the door, simply repeat. Eventually you will be able to bring him out of the cage door and into the room. Praise him frequently as you do so.

Give your parakeet a favorite treat after each session, and never be in a hurry when taming. Taming becomes easier once the parakeet realizes he has nothing to fear. Providing that you talk quietly, move slowly, and handle him gently, even adult parakeets can be tamed. Parakeets are both bold and inquisitive, and these factors work in your favor. Eventually your parakeet will perch on your finger and may even let you pet him or massage his head and neck.

TRAINING YOUR PARAKEET

Once you have hand-tamed your bird and he is always comfortable with you and trusts you, training can begin. Whether you are trying to train your bird to stay off the kitchen counter or to ride a toy scooter, you must use patience and rewards, not discipline. Not all rewards have to be treats—a head scratching and words of praise will also reward your bird for a job well done. Break the desired behavior down into cumulative steps, and work on them one at a time.

You may be surprised to find that as your bird figures out what is going on, he might even anticipate behavior, and he will certainly learn new ones more quickly. By choosing behaviors that are an extension of the bird's natural repertoire, you will make training an enjoyable game for both of you.

Using Positive Reinforcement

When training, it is essential to use positive reinforcement only, which is reinforcing desired behaviors using a positive reward. Rewards can be treats, favorite toys, or praise. *Never punish your parakeet.* Your parakeet must be able to trust you in order for training to be effective, and punishment destroys this necessary trust. Training should always be a positive experience.

Training "Step up" and "Step Down"

Training your parakeet to step up and step down on command are probably the most valuable lessons you can give your bird. They are

Treats can greatly help in the hand-taming process because they will entice your bird to come closer to your hand while also showing him that he can trust you.

important for your parakeet's safety because you can more easily retrieve him should he escape or get into a dangerous situation. These commands are also good training tools because they serve as foundations for more advanced training. Furthermore, these commands will be handy should you have to move your bird into a travel carrier or remove him from his cage during veterinary trips, cage cleaning, etc.

The step up and step down commands are really just extensions of hand-taming. Once your parakeet is comfortable being perched on your finger or hand, you will teach him to step onto your hand and off of it at the appropriate times based on the command.

As with hand-taming, lightly press your finger to your bird's chest or belly. This will force him to step up onto your finger. This time, as your bird begins to step onto your finger, say, "Step up." Reward your parakeet with treats and/or praise and repeat this action, always saying, "Step up" when your bird steps onto your finger or hand. Soon he will do this without much additional encouragement and will respond to the command without you having to press onto his chest or reward him.

Once you have hand-tamed your parakeet, you can move on to more advanced training.

THE GUIDE TO OWNING A PARAKEET

Always use positive reinforcement when training your parakeet, using treats, toys, or praise as rewards.

Training your parakeet to step down is very similar. At first, allow your parakeet to step off of your hand or finger when he wants to. When he does this, say, "Step down" and reward him with a treat or praise. Next, encourage him to step down yourself. Place your hand close to the place where you would like your parakeet to step onto (such as a perch, the floor, his cage floor, etc.) and say, "Step down." Do not force your parakeet off of your hand, but encourage him to step off by placing your hand where you want him to go. When he successfully steps off of your hand,

reward him with treats and praise. As with the step up command, your parakeet will soon understand that "step down" means that he should step off your hand, and he will eventually do this whenever you tell him to "step down."

Trick Training Your Parakeet

Although parakeets aren't renowned for their trick-training abilities, most parakeets can be taught a few tricks. Before you start trick training, pick a quiet room free of distractions where the training will take place. It's also a good idea to only have one person do the trick training,

The step up and step down commands are important training tools for your parakeet to master.

onto this fairly easily because it is an extension of his natural behavior to lift his feet.

To teach your parakeet to wave, have a treat or toy in your hand, hold it just beyond your bird's reach, and say, "Wave." If your parakeet knows the step up command well, you can also move your finger toward your bird, but instead of letting him perch on your finger, say, "Wave." Either way, praise or reward your bird for moving his foot, and repeat the process until your bird starts to connect the cue "wave" with the behavior of moving his foot.

Once he has mastered this move, try moving the treat in a wavelike

at least in the beginning. Have all supplies ready in this small room where training will be conducted, such as treats and a perch or stand. Also, remember to keep training sessions short. About 10 to 15 minutes is a decent amount of time for a training session, and if your parakeet seems tired or frustrated sooner than this, there is nothing wrong with shortening the session.

Begin with simple tricks. The easiest tricks for a parakeet to learn are tricks that are extensions of his normal behavior. A popular trick to teach parakeets is the wave, where your bird will extend his foot in a waving motion. Your parakeet should catch

It's a good idea to have only one person train your parakeet, at least in the beginning.

motion, saying, "Wave." Praise or reward your parakeet when he performs this wavelike motion. Eventually you will be able to eliminate the reward, and he will be able to perform the wave motion just by your verbal cue.

Another simple trick to teach your parakeet is nodding. Start by holding the treat above your parakeet's head, keeping it just out of reach. Say, "Nod," and move the treat in a downward motion, bringing it directly in front of his beak and then down past his head, so that his head follows the treat. Give him the treat as a reward and praise him. Repeat this process, using a treat to coax your bird to move his head downward. Once he understands this, use the treat to make him move his head down, back up, and then down again for a complete nod, saying "Nod" as you do so. Repeat this step several times. You may want to move back farther away from him each time if you notice that he is understanding what he is supposed to do when you say, "Nod." Soon you will be able to take away the treat entirely, and he will perform the nod just with your verbal cue.

Some parakeets may be responsive to more advanced tricks that are popular with parrots, such as basketball or stacking cups. If you decide to train your parakeet to perform these tricks, remember to break the trick

Teaching your parakeet to talk can be a fun activity for both you and your bird.

down into very small steps and to praise and reward frequently when your parakeet correctly performs the steps. Be extremely patient when teaching these more complicated tricks, and if your parakeet seems to get frustrated, have him perform an easier behavior that he does perform correctly, such as step up, and reward him for a job well done.

TEACHING YOUR PARAKEET TO TALK

Many parakeets talk frequently, mimicking many of the sounds and words that humans make, while others never talk at all. Teaching your parakeet to talk can be a fun activity for both you and your companion,

If you have a pair or group of parakeets, training will be most effective if their lessons are conducted separately.

but it is perfectly normal if your bird does not.

First, as with hand-taming, make sure there are no distractions, including mirrors. Begin with a single word, such as "hello," and repeat this many times. Never try to teach short sentences at first, but concentrate on that first word until your parakeet learns it. Once one word is vocalized, you can then move onto a second word, a third, and so on.

Once your parakeet has mastered several words, you can move on to phrases and response phrases, teaching them in the same manner. Repet-ition and patience are the keys to expanding your parakeet's vocabulary. Once your parakeet has developed the ability to talk, he will eventually begin to pick up words spoken by you and your family without even being taught these words.

If you have a pair or group of parakeets, speech lessons will have to be conducted separately. It is also more difficult to teach paired birds to talk because it is harder to overcome their natural desire to use their own language as they do with the other bird. They can still be taught to talk, however.

Parakeet Health Care

Clean, healthy living conditions and a varied, balanced diet go a long way toward providing your parakeet with a long, healthy life. However, even parakeets that receive the best of care can develop health problems or illnesses at some point in their lives.

Your parakeet should see his avian veterinarian for checkups at least once a year.

The best way to recognize a potential health problem in your parakeet is to pay close attention to your parakeet's normal behaviors. You should set aside time each day to study your parakeet, long enough to notice if he is not looking up to par. Check that he is eating well and generally moving about as normal. If you notice anything out of the ordinary with no obvious cause of the symptoms, you should take your parakeet to his avian veterinarian right way. Only a veterinarian can diagnose and treat these ailments, so it is important to find an avian veterinarian and take your companion to him or her within the first few days of obtaining your parakeet.

FINDING AN AVIAN VETERINARIAN

Finding an avian veterinarian is absolutely essential as part of the care of your parakeet. Besides regular checkups, the veterinarian will be available if and when something serious happens to your bird. Many veterinarians are not trained in care for "exotic" animals like the parakeet and may not be an expert in bird diseases and treatment. However, avian veterinarians are experts in bird care. Aside from being able to properly diagnose and treat avian ailments, these veterinarians can offer guidance and advice with issues such as training, feeding, and breeding.

Clean living conditions and a healthy diet go a long way toward keeping your parakeets in good health.

Finding an avian veterinarian is one of the most important things you will do for the care of your parakeet.

Providing your parakeet with plenty of toys and attention will help prevent any self-mutilating behaviors.

You should actually take your parakeet to his avian veterinarian within the first few days of obtaining him. This way you will be able to develop a relationship with your veterinarian. You should also take your parakeet for a checkup at least once a year.

If there is a zoo nearby, the veterinarians associated with it may be able to refer you to a colleague in private practice. Regular veterinarians should also be able to recommend a good avian veterinarian in the area, or the store or the breeder from which you obtained your parakeet can give you a reference.

COMMON PARAKEET HEALTH CONCERNS

Only your veterinarian can diagnose and treat any health problems in your parakeet, so if you suspect that your parakeet is suffering from some type of ailment or sickness, don't take the risk of diagnosing the problem yourself—take your parakeet to his avian veterinarian as soon as possible.

Arthritis

Parakeets who have arthritis will seem uncomfortable when moving certain joints, and moving these joints may seem to take a great deal of effort. Take your parakeet to the vet right away, because there are several ways to make this problem less painful to your bird. Your vet may suggest certain medications, changing the perches, or even changing the bird's diet if he is overweight.

Diarrhea

Your parakeet's droppings should consist of a solid green portion, white urates (on top of the green), and a clear liquid. Very loose droppings indicate a digestive problem that can range from mild/temporary to fatal.

The usual causes are fouled food, stale food, dusty or moldy seed, or unhygienic living conditions. Green, watery feces may indicate avian typhoid, which is highly contagious.

Isolate the bird, reduce the amount of green foods in the diet, and consult your veterinarian, who will probably administer antibiotics. All cage material, perches, and toys should be thoroughly cleaned.

Injuries and Bleeding

Parakeets are curious, active birds and may get minor scrapes or injuries. Minor bleeding caused by cuts or scrapes usually requires cleaning the area with antiseptic or the use of a styptic pencil. More serious wounds or broken bones require an immediate visit to the vet.

Self-Mutilation

Self-mutilation is a common problem in parrots, including parakeets. Often this is a behavioral problem triggered by boredom or lack of attention and socialization. If the parakeet's intelligent mind is not being stimulated enough, he may turn that frustration on himself by plucking his own feathers, picking at his flesh, or picking at his toenails.

If your parakeet suffers from self-mutilation, try offering him new toys or taking extra time to provide him with love and attention. If the problem still persists, this may signal an actual health problem not related to behavior. Take your parakeet to his avian veterinarian as soon as possible in this case, because the self-mutila-

It's important to pay close attention to your parakeet's normal behaviors so that you may recognize a change that could indicate illness.

If you keep your parakeet's living area clean, there is little risk of an infestation of red mites.

tion may indicate a serious medical problem.

Illness and Disease

Only your avian veterinarian should diagnose and treat potential illnesses or diseases. However, you can be aware of some of the symptoms that may signal common illnesses. If you notice that your parakeet's feathers are fluffed up with his eyes closed, he could be ill. Also look out for watery discharge around the nose and eyes, weight loss, fatigue, or breathing difficulties.

Aspergillosis

Aspergillosis is a fungal disease that commonly affects a parakeet's lungs. Symptoms are rapid breathing, difficulty breathing, and wheezing. Keeping your bird in clean, well- ventilated areas can help prevent this disease, but if you suspect that your

parakeet is suffering from aspergillosis, make an appointment with your parakeet's vet.

Polyoma Virus

Polyoma virus usually affects young birds, though adult birds can carry the disease and pass it to their young. Signs of this disease include weakness or fatigue, abnormal feathers, paralysis, and an enlarged abdomen. You should definitely have your veterinarian check your parakeet (or any birds you have) for this disease. There is no cure or treatment, but there is currently a vaccine.

Psittacosis

Psittacosis is not particularly common, but it is highly contagious and can even be transmitted to humans. The disease is transmitted through droppings and discharge. Parakeets who suffer from this disease may have

THE GUIDE TO OWNING A PARAKEET

abnormally colored droppings or show signs of weight loss and fatigue. Humans who suffer from this disease appear to have flu symptoms. There are medications available for both humans and parakeets who suffer from this disease, so if you suspect either people in your home or birds in your home of suffering from this illness, it's best to take care of it immediately.

Psittacine Beak and Feather Disease

Psittacine Beak and Feather Disease is highly contagious among birds and is often fatal. Symptoms include beak lesions, feather loss, and a weakened condition.

Pacheco's Disease

Pacheco's Disease is a highly contagious disease. Strict quarantine is the best preventative measure against this disease. It is a viral infection that affects the liver, and it usually isn't diagnosed until death.

Parasites

The most common parasites of parakeets are the red mite, the feather mite, and the leg or face mite. Mites are tiny arthropods barely visible to the eye. Some live on the actual host itself, while some live elsewhere but still attack the host.

Red Mite
(Dermanyssus gallinae)

These mites are usually introduced

When you first bring home a new bird, you should place him in an isolation cage in order to ensure that your original birds don't catch any illnesses he could be carrying.

by new birds, wild birds, or live poultry in the area. They live in crevices of woodwork, coming out at night to feed on the blood of their host. When high levels of infestation are reached, the bird scratches and loses sleep.

Old and young birds succumb more easily. They may die from anemia or from secondary infections caused from scratching. Brooding hens may abandon a nest when infestation is high. Feather plucking may commence, which may then become habitual.

Contact your veterinarian immediately if you suspect your bird has these mites. Most likely, cages will need to be sprayed and scrubbed and all nesting material and perches will need to be discarded. If hygiene is as it should be, there is little risk of heavy infestation.

Feather Mite
(Ornithonyssus sylvirum)

Feather mites live and reproduce on the host itself. Consequently, they are far easier to control. See your avian veterinarian as soon as possible for treatment.

Scalyface and Leg Mite
(Knemidocpotes pilae)

These mites are characterized by horny growths on parts of the face, the upper mandible, and legs. See your avian veterinarian as soon as possible. Treatment in mild cases is by application of liquid paraffin painted on the affected surface. Make regular inspections of the bird after treatment to check for reinfestation.

Household Dangers

Most if not all cleansers, disinfectants, and other household chemicals are poisonous to birds and should not be used around them. Especially dangerous are chemicals designed to kill insects.

Many common houseplants are also toxic, not only to birds but to all animals, including humans. It's best to consider any houseplant poisonous unless you are certain it is not.

Non-stick cookware is also extremely dangerous and potentially deadly. When heated, the non-stick material gives off fumes that are toxic to birds. Never cook using non-stick cookware while your bird is in the room or house. Perhaps even easier is to make sure all of your cookware and appliances are not made from non-stick material.

ISOLATION CAGES

A common cause of spreading infection is the introduction of recently acquired birds immediately into the cage of your original birds. If you have other birds, you should quarantine new birds when you first bring them home. It is not enough simply to put the new bird in another cage; isolation cages are to be as far away from the regular stock as possible. Allow at least ten days to pass for an illness to present itself if possible. If the new bird seems healthy after ten days, you can introduce him to your other birds.

Breeding Parakeets

Parakeets are prolific breeders in captivity. Because parakeets breed so freely, many parakeet owners choose to breed their pets. However, this is not a decision that should be taken lightly. In fact, most people should not breed their parakeets. Breeding is a serious decision that produces

Before breeding your parakeets, make sure you have new homes or extra space in your own home to house the babies.

It's best to allow your parakeets to pair naturally or to buy a proven pair that has already produced babies together.

living, breathing birds that will need homes and loving care. Successful breeding is also complicated and difficult for inexperienced breeders.

THINGS TO CONSIDER BEFORE BREEDING

First and most importantly, you need to consider where the babies will live. Do you have enough space, time, and resources to house them yourself, or do you have other people willing to provide forever homes for all of the babies? If you do not, you should not breed your parakeet.

Second, you should consider whether you can afford to breed your parakeet. Many people assume they will make money from breeding, but in actuality, it can be expensive, espe-cially if you plan to hand-feed your babies. Veterinary costs, food and housing expenses, and other supplies can become quite expensive in the long run, so you should be certain that you can afford all of these necessities involved with breeding.

Finally, time is a necessity. If you don't have the time to provide the extra care and attention necessary, you probably should not breed your parakeets.

If you do, in fact, have the time, money, resources, and potential homes for the babies, and you have carefully made the decision to breed your parakeet, you can probably have a successful breeding plan if you follow the correct steps and go into breeding fully prepared.

PAIRING AND COMPATIBILITY

One male parakeet and one female parakeet do not necessarily equal a pair. Like humans, parakeets will choose their partners themselves and may not agree with the mates you choose for them. Therefore, the best way to ensure success is to allow the birds to pair naturally.

However, you can also buy a proven pair, meaning that they have already produced babies with each other. By obtaining a proven pair, you know they are compatible. This depends completely on the honesty of the seller, however. If you decide to go this route, get a guarantee in writing, which any reputable breeder or store will be more than happy to provide.

BREEDING CONDITION

If your parakeet pair is in good breeding condition, it means that the pair is in a fit condition, showing good health, excellent overall feather condition, and being neither overweight nor underweight. Reproduction and chick rearing places a great strain on birds, so it is essential that they have as much aviary flight time as possible prior to the breeding period and that they have a very healthy, nutritious diet.

When he is in peak condition, the male's beak will be a vivid blue, and

When she is in peak condition, the female parakeet's cere will turn from pale to rich brown with a crusty texture.

he will be constantly active and on the go. The female's cere will turn from pale to a rich brown with a crusty texture. She will also start gnawing at bits of wood, an indication that she is ready to nest.

BREEDING AGE

The optimum years of breeding for parakeets are usually between one and four years of age, though the male tends to have a longer breeding life than the hen. It is also advised that a hen should not be allowed more than two clutches in a season. While she is capable of having more, it is often the case that the number of eggs is fewer and the chicks are not as strong. Egg laying and rearing of the chicks takes a high toll on the female's body, and she needs plenty of time to rebuild her strength.

MATING

Courtship in parakeets is undertaken through mutual preening between the pair, much chattering between the two, the male feeding the hen, and the male displaying himself to the female. A small bit of squabbling may take place. If this seems to be truly aggressive, it might be best to separate them, because they may be incompatible.

HOUSING YOUR BREEDERS
Cage Breeders

A cage for breeding parakeets does

Cage breeding greatly simplifies the process and allows you to carefully monitor progress.

THE GUIDE TO OWNING A PARAKEET

Parakeets display courtship by mutual preening, frequent chattering, and the male feeding the hen.

not need to be very different from a regular cage. Because two birds are involved, it should be roomy, and it will require space for attaching a nest box.

With cage breeding, you can monitor progress and change easily. Checking the nest boxes, banding babies, and keeping track of each pair is greatly simplified when there is only one pair per cage.

Colony Breeders

Because they are also very sociable birds, parakeets can be bred safely in a colony system. This requires a fairly large aviary, however, because you will need separate nest boxes and territories for each breeding pair.

It is essential that you make sure you have an equal number of males and females, because unpaired birds can cause problems for the nesting pairs. It is even better if you introduce the birds after they have paired.

Nest Boxes

Parakeets will accept a variety of styles and sizes of nest boxes. The nest box should be placed so that when opened, it is slightly above the level of bedding. It should be large enough to accommodate a pair of parakeets and between four and eight chicks comfortably.

The access hole should be just large enough for the parents to enter and exit, because parakeets like secure,

It is very important for baby parakeets to receive a healthy, nutritious diet.

protected nesting sites. A wooden ladder should be secured on the internal side of the access hole, and a landing perch should be placed just below the entrance hole.

EGG LAYING AND INCUBATION

Approximately nine or ten days after mating, the hen will lay four to eight eggs every other day. If no eggs have appeared by the 18th day, the mating was probably not successful. Assuming all is well, the hen will commence incubation after the first egg is laid.

Parakeet eggs are white and about 3/4 x 5/8 inches in size (18 x 15 mm). When first laid, they are translucent, but this changes to opaque after a few days. Should this change to a darker grayish color, a problem may be present.

The incubation period of the eggs is 18 days, after which the chick will use a horn-shaped growth, known as its egg tooth, on its beak to cut a hole in the shell by rotating itself in the shell.

Although parakeets are usually very tolerant of having their nest boxes inspected after eggs have been laid, such viewings should be restricted to once a day. At such times, you should take the opportunity to remove any built-up debris in the nest. The best time to inspect the next boxes is during the morning when the hen is out of the box.

The chicks will be ready to leave the nest at about three or four weeks of

Chicks will not be ready to leave the nest until they are about three to four weeks of age.

age but will continue to return to the nest at night for maybe a week or two more, assuming the hen will let them.

SPECIAL FEEDING INSTRUCTIONS

Once the chicks hatch, the only food they get is what the parents bring to them, and this ultimately comes from what you feed the parents. The regular daily diet of your parakeets should already be varied and balanced, but during breeding you should take special care to ensure that the birds receive enough fresh fruits, vegetables, extra eggs, and soft foods.

Have an experienced breeder or veterinarian show you how to hand-feed baby parakeets, and acquire a great deal of supervised practice before handling this task on your own.

Hand-Feeding the Babies

If you wish to learn to hand-feed babies, you should enlist the aid of an experienced breeder. Although an enjoyable task, hand-feeding a large number of baby birds can be quite tedious and nerve-wracking.

Inexperienced owners should *not* undertake this task without a lot of training. The actual process of getting the food into the chick is not difficult to master, but knowing how to spot medical problems before they get too serious is not something you can learn from a few paragraphs in a book. By spending time with an experienced hand-feeder, you will pick up the information that you need to raise healthy babies.

Once you are satisfied that the youngsters are feeding themselves, they can then be taken from their parents and caged with others of the same age.

Resources

ORGANIZATIONS

American Federation of Aviculture, Inc.
P.O. Box 7312
N. Kansas City, MO 64116
Telephone: (816) 421-2473
Fax: (816) 421-3214
E-mail: afaoffice@aol.com
www.AFAbirds.org

Avicultural Society of America
Secretary: Helen Hanson
E-mail: info@asabirds.org
www.asabirds.org

Budgerigar Association of America
Secretary: Kerry Laverty
E-mail: pro@applink.net
www.budgerigarassociation.com

The American Budgerigar Society
Secretary: Diane Ingram
E-mail: abssecretary@cs.com
www.abs1.org

PUBLICATIONS

Bird Talk Magazine
3 Burroughs
Irvine, CA 92618
Telephone: (949) 855-8822
Fax: (949) 855-3045
www.animalnetwork.com/birdtalk/default.asp

Budgerigar World
E-mail: budgerigarworld@msn.com
www.budgerigarworld.com

Winged Wisdom Magazine
Birds n Ways
39760 Calle Bellagio
Temecula, CA 92592
Telephone: (909) 303-9376
www.birdsnways.com

INTERNET RESOURCES

Budgerigars Galore
(www.budgerigars.co.uk)
Budgerigars Galore offers a variety of information on topics like nutrition, breeding, and health. The site also provides tips for beginners and links to other budgie pages.

VETERINARY RESOURCES

Association of Avian Veterinarians (AAV)
P.O. Box 811720
Boca Raton, FL 33481-1720
Telephone: (561) 393-8901
Fax: (561) 393-8902
E-mail: AAVCTRLOFC@aol.com
www.aav.org

EMERGENCY RESOURCES AND RESCUE ORGANIZATIONS

ASPCA Animal Poison Control Center
Telephone: (888) 426-4435
E-mail: napcc@aspca.org (for nonemergency, general information only)
www.apcc.aspca.org

Bird Hotline
P.O. Box 1411
Sedona, AZ 86339-1411
E-mail: birdhotline@birdhotline.com
www.birdhotline.com

Index